I0409626

U.S. DEPARTMENT OF HOMELAND SECURITY

FISCAL YEAR 2013

CHEMICAL STOCKPILE EMERGENCY
PREPAREDNESS PROGRAM (CSEPP)

COOPERATIVE AGREEMENT GUIDANCE

JUNE 2012

Table of Contents

This page intentionally left blank.

FY 2013 CHEMICAL EMERGENCY STOCKPILE PREPAREDNESS PROGRAM (CSEPP)

FUNDING OPPORTUNITY ANNOUNCEMENT (FOA)

OVERVIEW INFORMATION

Issued By
U.S. Department of Homeland Security (DHS): Federal Emergency Management Agency (FEMA)

Catalogue of Federal Domestic Assistance (CFDA) Number
97.040

CFDA Title
Chemical Stockpile Emergency Preparedness Program (CSEPP)

Funding Opportunity Announcement Title
Fiscal Year (FY) 2013 Chemical Emergency Stockpile Preparedness Program

Authorizing Authority for Program
Public Law 99-145 (50 U.S.C. 1521), Destruction of Existing Stockpile of Lethal Chemical Agents and Munitions
44 Code of Federal Regulations, Part 13, Uniform Administration Requirements for Grants and Cooperative Agreements to State, Tribal and local governments
DHS/FEMA and the U.S. Army CSEPP MOU, 23 March 2004

Appropriation Authority for Program
The Department of Defense Authorization Act of 1986, Title 14, Part B, Section 1412
Public Law 99-145, 50 USC 1521

FOA Number
Not applicable

Key Dates and Time
Application Start Date: Published date of the FY 2013 CSEPP CA Guidance.
Budget Negotiations Date: Not later than 08/01/2012
Application Submission Deadline Date: 08/15/2012 at 11:59:59 p.m. EDT
Anticipated Funding Selection Date: 10/01/2012
Anticipated Award Date: 10/01/2012

Intergovernmental Review
Is an intergovernmental review required?

☒ Yes ☐ No

Executive Order 12372 requires Grantees from State and local units of government or other organizations providing services within a State to submit a copy of the application to the State Single Point of Contact (SPOC), if one exists, and if this program has been selected for review by the State. Grantees must contact their State SPOC to determine if the program has been selected for State review. Executive Order 12372 can be referenced at http://www.archives.gov/federal-register/codification/executive-order/12372.html. The names and addresses of the SPOCs are listed on the Office of Management and Budget's (OMB's) home page available at: www.whitehouse.gov/sites/default/files/omb/assets/grants/spoc.pdf.

FOA EXECUTIVE SUMMARY

Program Type
Select the applicable program type: This award is a Cooperative Agreement due to the substantial involvement of both the Department of Army and the Federal Emergency Management Agency as described in Part I, Funding Opportunity Description.

☒ New ☐ Continuing ☐ One-time New or Continuing

Date of origin for program: 1989

Opportunity Category
Select the applicable opportunity category:

☐ Discretionary ☐ Mandatory ☐ Competitive (OPSG only) ☒ Non-competitive

☐ Sole Source

Application Process
Refer to Part X for the CSEPPWebCA application process.

Eligible Applicants and Cooperative Agreement Applications:
The eligible States contain the emergency planning zones surrounding the Army stockpiles of unitary chemical warfare agent as bulk chemicals and munitions. Local governments participate as Subgrantees under their State's application. A new application is required for each fiscal year.
The following entities are eligible to apply directly to FEMA under this solicitation:

☒ Governments of the State of Colorado and the Commonwealth of Kentucky.

For additional information, see the *Eligibility Criteria* section of this FOA.

Type of Funding Instrument
Select the applicable funding instrument:

☐ Grant ☒ Cooperative Agreement

Cost Share or Match
Select the applicable requirement:

☐ Cost Match ☐ Cost Share ☒ None Required

Maintenance of Effort
Is there a Maintenance of Effort (MOE) requirement?

☐ Yes ☒ No

Management and Administration

Management and Administration costs are covered in individual line item Benchmarks for Administration and indirect costs. Refer to the tables in Part IV for allowable costs.

FULL FOA

I. Funding Opportunity Description

Program Overview

History of the Chemical Stockpile Emergency Preparedness Program (CSEPP)

In 1985, Congress directed the Department of Defense (DoD) to dispose of its lethal unitary (pre-mixed) chemical agents and munitions while providing "maximum protection for the environment, the general public, and the personnel involved." In 1987, the U.S. Army (Army) released a draft Emergency Response Concept Plan (ERCP), which presented a basis for the development of local emergency response programs and examined various methods of emergency planning. The Army also prepared a Chemical Stockpile Disposal Implementation Plan and requested funds to implement enhanced emergency preparedness on-post and off-post for all eight chemical stockpile sites. FEMA joined the Army in implementing CSEPP through a Memorandum of Understanding (MOU) signed in August 1988. This MOU was reaffirmed in 1993 and revised in 1997 and 2004.

CSEPP is a project conducted under the chemical demilitarization program, a major defense acquisition program executed by the U.S. Army. CSEPP augments the Army's installation chemical accident and incident response capability. The Army is responsible for programming and budgeting validated CSEPP requirements as developed by the State and local governments and validated by FEMA. The Deputy Assistant Secretary of the Army for Eliminating Chemical Weapons (DASA [ECW]) is responsible for overseeing the CSEPP execution, to include coordination with Congress, FEMA, and the Citizen Advisory Commissions. The Chemical Materials Agency executes the day-to-day management of CSEPP, to include upgrading on-post response capabilities; developing on-post preparedness plans; conducting on-post training; automation; and integrating on- and off-post capabilities.

FEMA is responsible for off-post emergency preparedness and works with the States and local governments in the development of preparedness plans, conducting necessary training, administering cooperative agreements, and upgrading response capabilities. Off-post efforts include command and control, public awareness of protective actions, communication, and alert notification systems (e.g., computer hardware and software, telephone and radio upgrades, sirens, and tone alert radios). FEMA assists the States and local governments in planning and validating their CSEPP requirements and distributes funds to the States under cooperative agreements. The States and local governments execute plans to protect the public and provide financial and performance reports, addressing the capability improvements realized through those funds.

While the likelihood of a chemical stockpile incident with off-post consequences is considered remote, the Army and FEMA recognize that the impact of such an event could be significant. CSEPP Strategic Plan states the basic goal of CSEPP is "to mitigate the effects of an accident to the maximum extent practicable." Thus, CSEPP has two basic objectives:

1. To establish and enhance emergency preparedness in nearby communities, including community alert and warning systems and protective action strategies.

2. To institute protective measures and hazard mitigation strategies at the chemical stockpile sites (the Army installations) to lessen the vulnerability of the storage structures and their contents to any internally or externally generated accidents.

CSEPP National Benchmarks (CNB)

In 1993, the Army and FEMA defined a set of National Benchmarks to guide the development and assessment of CSEPP capabilities as identified in CSEPP Policy Paper No.18. In 2000, these Benchmarks were updated and include 12 distinct capabilities. These Benchmarks are similar to and essentially capture the disaster preparedness capabilities of the National Fire Protection Association (NFPA) 1600 standards. These capabilities are a key tool in the planning, programming, and budgeting of CSEPP efforts at the installations and with the States and local governments. In addition, these capabilities are used to assess and report the status of CSEPP efforts at and around the two chemical stockpile sites within the United States. The CSEPP Joint Army/FEMA Strategic Plan incorporates the National Benchmarks as the core long-term goals of the program.

The CSEPP National Benchmarks are as follows:
1. Administrative support (ADM) for each installation, State, and immediate response zone (IRZ) and protective action zone (PAZ) counties.

2. Functioning alert and notification system (A&N) for each installation and IRZ.

3. Functioning automated data processing system (ADP) connecting critical installation facilities, on-post emergency operations centers (EOCs), off-post EOCs, joint information centers (JICs), and State EOCs.

4. Functioning communications system (COM) for IRZ counties and installations, as well as between EOCs, military installations, JICs, and States.

5. Coordinated plans (COP) conforming to established CSEPP guidance for each installation, State, IRZ, and PAZ county are to be updated as guidance is revised or as the jurisdictions' circumstances change.

6. Functioning EOCs for each installation and IRZ county.

7. An exercise program (EX) that is consistent with the approved exercise policy of the Exercise Working Group.

8. A medical program (MED) for off-post medical preparation and response to a CSEPP incident/accident.

9. Personnel (PER), such as CSEPP coordinators, public information/public affairs officers, planners, and ADP specialists, to support CSEPP activities on the installation and in the State and IRZ counties.

10. Protective action strategy (PRO) conforming to established CSEPP guidance for each jurisdiction.

11. A public outreach/education program (POE) for public information and education.

12. Training programs (TNG) consistent with the FEMA State Training Plan (for off-post jurisdictions) and Army certification requirements (for on-post installations), and maintained proficiency of emergency services providers/responders and CSEPP staff, as defined and measured by CSEPP guidance.

CSEPP Life Cycle Cost Estimate

The State of Colorado and the Commonwealth of Kentucky maintain a CSEPP Life Cycle Cost Estimate (LCCE) outlining the cost estimates for all anticipated programmatic requirements. The LCCE is a component of the overall DoD planning, programming, budgeting, and execution process.

Success Story

CSEPP activities are an extension of DHS/FEMA's mission "to lead America to prepare for, prevent, respond to, and recover from disasters." CSEPP's mission is to "enhance existing local, installation, tribal, State, and Federal capabilities to protect the health and safety of the public, work force, and environment from the effects of a chemical accident or incident involving the U.S. Army chemical stockpile." This mission is accomplished in CSEPP through partnerships (in accordance with the whole community approach) with the Army, Federal department and agencies, states, local governments, volunteer organizations, and private industry. CSEPP's mission aligns with FEMA and Army goals by protecting off-post civilians and employees who work on one of the two Army depots that store chemical warfare agents from the unlikely event of a chemical accident or incident. The Army is fulfilling its mission to eliminate aging chemical munitions and chemical warfare materials. This objective is in accordance with international treaties and national policies.

The unique Federal responsibility to CSEPP communities has had an added benefit: CSEPP communities are better prepared to respond to all hazards, regardless of cause. By utilizing appropriated funds provided by the Army, at the direction of Congress, FEMA has helped CSEPP communities ensure that, regardless of the cause, emergency managers can determine when an emergency is occurring; assess and predict its impact; broadcast effective messages to inform the affected population; determine appropriate public health and safety strategies; and, if required, evacuate and shelter those at risk. The increased capability of local officials to protect the public will remain a CSEPP legacy long after the stockpile is successfully destroyed and CSEPP's mission ends.

Two key policies have guided successful management of CSEPP. First, assessments based upon defensible scientific methods and quantitative reasoning has guided all procurement and management decisions. Second, and just as important, is CSEPP's primary goal: Protect the public from potential incidents involving military installations that house lethal chemical agents and munitions. The collective commitment of CSEPP participants to that goal has made the communities surrounding each of the stockpile sites safer than they were before the Program began.

As of January 23, 2012[1], 89.75 percent of the original stockpile has been destroyed with no negative impacts on the communities surrounding the chemical stockpile locations.

Linkage to the Quadrennial Homeland Security Review (QHSR)
As previously addressed in the CSEPP History, the goal of CSEPP is to mitigate the effects of an unlikely incident from the chemical stockpile. CSEPP has two objectives, to establish and enhance emergency preparedness and to institute protective measures and hazard mitigation strategies at the chemical stockpile sites.

In addition, CSEPP's specific mission contributes to Mission 5: Ensuring Resilience to Disasters.

- Mission 5: Ensuring Resilience to Disasters
  - Goal 5.1: Mitigate Hazards
  - Goal 5.2: Enhance Preparedness
  - Goal 5.3: Ensure Effective Emergency Response
  - Goal 5.4: Rapidly Recover

For additional details on the QHSR Report, please refer to http://www.dhs.gov/xabout/gc_1208534155450.shtm.

II. Funding Information

Award Amounts, Important Dates, and Extensions
Available funding for this FOA: For FY 2013, the President's budget submission for Chemical Agents and Munitions Destruction, Defense includes a request for approximately $18,263,000 to be distributed by DHS/FEMA under Cooperative Agreements to the two States remaining in the program. DHS/FEMA will allocate based on approved and validated requirements contained in CSEPP Programmatic Guidance www.orise.orau.gov/csepp/documents/planning/csepp-planning-guidance.pdf.

---

[1]http://www.cma.army.mil/verticalmetricswindow.aspx?graph=Agent&desc=Agent%20Destruction%20Status

Period of Performance
Is an extension to the period of performance permitted?

☒ Yes ☐ No

The period of performance for all CSEPP Cooperative Agreements begins October 1, with the end date of the performance period established by respective FEMA components after evaluating the scope of work provided by the Grantees. Extensions to the period of performance will be considered only though formal requests to FEMA with specific and compelling justifications as to why an extension is required. Refer to the Extension Policy narrative in Part X for additional information.

III.   **Eligibility Information**

Eligibility Criteria
Applications are accepted from the State of Colorado and the Commonwealth of Kentucky. The eligible jurisdictions are at risk from the Army stockpiles of unitary chemical warfare agent and bulk chemicals and munitions.

IV.   **Funding Restrictions**

Restrictions on Use of Award Funds
DHS/FEMA cooperative agreement funds may only be used for the purpose set forth in the cooperative agreement, and must be consistent with the statutory authority for the award. Cooperative agreement funds may not be used for matching funds for other Federal grants/cooperative agreements, lobbying, or intervention in Federal regulatory or adjudicatory proceedings. In addition, Federal funds may not be used to sue the Federal government or any other government entity.

In developing CSEPP budgets, consider the following:

- Only request funding for salary and benefits of filled positions; do not request funding for positions that are vacant at the time of CA submission. This step is critical for Grantees or Subgrantees that are requesting reimbursement for indirect costs based on salaries and benefits.

- Cost for salary and benefits of filled positions should be obtained from the State or county personnel office. This cost should include cost of living projections based on approved legislation.

- Requests to fund any vacant position must be documented in the agency explanation section to include a projected hire date, salary, and percentage of time devoted to CSEPP. An employee work plan must also be completed and submitted.

- At a minimum, salaries must be reported on a budget line item indicating "Personnel," and fringe benefits must be reported on a line item indicating "Fringe Benefits." Positions may be entered on separate line items if desired. In either case, the following data is required for each CSEPP position and will be entered in the Agency Explanation section: title/position, salary, and percentage of time attributable to CSEPP.

- Travel and per diem cost should reflect actual travel cost projections for FY 2013.

- Base Operating Cost (BOC) items are annual and recurring operation and maintenance requirements.

  - Adjustments for BOC items more than 10 percent above the previous year cost amount will require justification in the Agency Explanation section of the Add/Edit Funding Requests function in CSEPPWebCA.

  - Reallocation of funds from a BOC item can result in a decrease in the requested funding level of that line item and future cost estimates.

  - Justifications for new BOC items are required to be included in the Agency Explanation section of the Add/Edit Funding Requests worksheet in CSEPPWebCA. The Grantee and the CSEPP Regional Program Manager will document their concurrence/non-concurrence in their respective remarks sections.

- Items involving new equipment or equipment replacement must be identified as complete systems rather than fragmented or non-referenced parts of a system (e.g., tactical radio system replacement, EOC server replacement, etc.) and prioritized for consideration with appropriate justification and cost data.

- Grantees and Subgrantees using CSEPP funds to support emergency communications activities should comply with the FY 2012 SAFECOM Guidance for Emergency Communication Grants, including provisions on technical standards that ensure and enhance interoperable communications. Emergency communications activities include the purchase of interoperable communications equipment and technologies such as voice-over-internet protocol bridging or gateway devices. Digital voice systems, including radios, must be compliant with the Project 25 (P25) suite of standards, capable of AES encryption, and in accordance with the Grantees' Statewide Interoperability Communications Plan. SAFECOM guidance can be found at http://www.safecomprogram.gov. Project 25 guidance can be found at http://www.project25.org.

- For purposes of determining which type of appropriated funding should be requested for new equipment or equipment replacement, the following applies: if the totality of the equipment in the line item is valued at $250,000 or less, request O&M appropriated funds; if the totality of the equipment in the line item is valued at more than $250,000, request Procurement appropriated funds.

- For purposes of defining "Equipment" the following definition from 44 CFR, Chapter 13.32 applies: equipment means tangible, non-expendable, personal property having a useful life of more than one year and an acquisition cost of $5,000 or more per unit.

Matching contributions and in-kind contributions must follow the requirements of 44 CFR 13.24 http://ecfr.gpoaccess.gov/cgi/t/text/text-idx?c=ecfr&sid=7b181e872e92de7853ba60b7954445cb&rgn=div8&view=text&node=44:1.0.1.1.14.3.12.5&idno=44.

As with other FEMA grant programs, CSEPP cannot provide funding for personnel, administrative or other costs incurred during the liquidation period.

The following table provides guidance on allowable costs within each Benchmark.

	Allowable costs include...	Unallowable costs include...	Cost apportionment items...
General Rules for All Benchmarks	Refer to items specified in OMB Circular A-87: http://www.whitehouse.gov/omb/circulars/a087/a87_2004.html and 44 CFR Part 13; Negotiated costs requirements necessary for CSEPP response capabilities and allowed by regulation.	Refer to items specified in OMB Circular A-87: http://www.whitehouse.gov/omb/circulars/a087/a87_2004.html and 44 CFR Part 13; Direct funding to host counties; Preprogramming funds to cost overruns, without prior Region approval; Assigning liability to CSEPP for costs greater than an approved budget item.	Shared costs that contribute to CSEPP capabilities as well as other required emergency programs. Requests for apportionment of allowable cost items must be approved by the Regional Assistance Officer and the CSEPP Regional Program Manager.
Administration (ADM)	Costs for office operations and maintenance for all CSEPP Benchmarks, except medical. business cards for 100 percent CSEPP funded personnel; Telephone charges and associated utilities such as gas, electric, and water; Supplies and expendable equipment with a useful life of one year or less and an acquisition cost of less than $5,000; Contracted services including contracted personnel not attributable to another CNB; Travel and per diem for all CSEPP purposes except medical; One leased vehicle for State government CSEPP travel; One leased vehicle for IRZ County CSEPP travel; Vehicle operations and maintenance; Any allowable item not covered by another CSEPP National Benchmark category definition.	Stationery, subscriptions to magazines and newspapers, uniforms, and membership dues; Payments for copyrights; Payments for lobbying costs; Mileage and per diem rates in excess of approved local, State, or Federal rates; A vehicle for CSEPP emergency response by EOC staff; Note: Vehicles for decontamination and screening response (such as equipment trailers, trailer mounted decontamination systems, or prime movers for these trailers) may be allowable and should be requested under the Protective Action Benchmark. A leased vehicle for PAZ or host county CSEPP travel; Travel to non-CSEPP events; Compliance with the Civil Rights and Americans with Disabilities Acts.	
Alert and Notification (A&N)	Costs, including contracts, for the planning, locating, and acquisition of equipment and/or leasing, installation, testing, operating, and maintaining of CSEPP public alert and notification systems; Note: Systems include indoor/outdoor alerting devices such as sirens and public address speakers, tone alert radios, telephone based warning systems, hot line ring down systems, and other audible warning devices.	Weather warning capabilities except weather alert radios used as tone alert radios/indoor alerting systems under an agreement between the Grantee or Subgrantee and the National Weather Service. Systems and equipment that do not comply with the FY 2012 SAFECOM Guidance for Emergency Communication Grants, including provisions on technical standards that ensure and enhance interoperable communications, the Project 25 (P25) suite of standards, or the Statewide Interoperability Communications Plan (see page 9 for more information).	

	Allowable costs include...	Unallowable costs include...	Cost apportionment items...
Automated Data Processing System (ADP)	Costs, including contracts, for planning, equipment acquisition and/or leasing, software acquisition, installation, testing, and maintenance.	Hardware, software, and automation equipment/maintenance that does not support CSEPP.	Operating and maintaining automation systems for all Benchmarks that support CSEPP as well as other operations.
Communication System (COM)	Costs, including contracts, for planning, locating, equipment acquisition and/or leasing, installation, testing, operating, and maintaining communications services for direct support of emergency response operations; Network linkage communications, dedicated non-public telephone systems, mobile and portable radio systems, pagers, and base stations	Communication systems not specifically required by CSEPP or systems supporting areas outside of CSEPP response communities; Cell phones and user charges for non-CSEPP employees. Cost of more than one communications device per person. Systems and equipment that do not comply with the FY 2012 SAFECOM Guidance for Emergency Communication Grants, including provisions on technical standards that ensure and enhance interoperable communications, the Project 25 (P25) suite of standards, or the Statewide Interoperability Communications Plan (see page 9 for more information).	Radio communications systems, pagers, mobile communications van, upgrade of existing State or county communications systems, cellular telephones and user charges, and communications equipment maintenance supporting CSEPP as part of a public safety response network.
Coordinated Plans (COP)	Costs, including contracts, for developing, maintaining, integrating, and coordinating CSEPP plans to include planning for recovery and reentry.		
Emergency Operations Center (EOC)	Costs, including contracts, for planning, equipment acquisition and/or leasing, installing, testing, operating, and maintaining an EOC facility.		Mobile EOCs, EOC medical equipment beyond general first-aid, alternate EOCs and equipment, and routine custodial, maintenance and utility costs. If CSEPP has created an additional cost above previously in-place service, justification must be provided for inclusion in the CSEPP budget.
Exercise Program (EX)	Costs, including contracts, for planning, conducting, and evaluating exercises of emergency preparedness plans and procedures in response to a simulated chemical agent incident/accident; Reimbursement for exercise expenses, such as meals and travel costs for volunteer participants, as specified in the Programmatic Guidance and Exercise Blue Book.		
Medical (MED)	CSEPP costs for planning and operating medical services and operating public health/medical support facilities; Acquisition of medical equipment and supplies specific to a CSEPP response; Salaries and benefits directly associated with the CSEPP medical program; All travel, contractual costs, minor construction, or renovation costs associated with the CSEPP medical program;	Construction of fixed decontamination facilities or decontamination rooms inside hospitals; Mobile decontamination units for hospital use. Conversion of mobile units no longer required for field use to fixed hospital installations may be considered on a case-by-case basis; Additional personnel to perform decontamination; Equipment, i.e., respirators, defibrillators; Development of new CSEPP medical training courses.	

	Allowable costs include…	Unallowable costs include…	Cost apportionment items…
	Indirect costs associated with the CSEPP medical program; Training and exercising of personnel associated with the CSEPP medical program.		
Personnel (PER)	Salaries and fringe benefits for full and part time State and local government employees covered by a State or local merit plan. Salaries and benefits for CSEPP funded positions with approved work plans up until the end of the peformance period. **Exception:** Salaries and benefits directly associated with the medical program are to be reported in the Medical Benchmark. Note: CSEPP positions, with approval of the State and CSEPP Regional Program Manager, may be reassigned to achieve the most benefit to the program. Note: CSEPP will only pay cost of living or appropriately scheduled raises for CSEPP funded personnel. A copy of the statute that approves the cost of living raise or other documentation for the salary increase must be submitted to the CSEPP Regional Program Manager.	Reallocation of salary and benefit funds or other personnel expenses without prior approval. Additional CSEPP FTEs. Salaries and benefits for any positions after the end of the performance period, including during the liquidation period. Note: Adjustments within approved positions are allowable, as long as there is no net FTE increase.	
Protective Actions (PRO)	Equipment only for public and private-sector responders whose agencies or organizations have a defined role in CSEPP as delineated in the jurisdiction's plan. This includes designated CSEPP hospitals. Note: Equipment purchased with CSEPP funds shall be appropriate for the response activities specified in CSEPP programmatic and planning guidance. Costs, including contracts, for evacuation planning; shelter-in-place planning; sheltering improvements by expedient measures, permanent enhancements, or pressurization if required and approved; evacuation activities; reception center activities; mass care facilities; decontamination activities. Costs for personal protective equipment acquisition Equipment acquisition for operating traffic and access control points, including: • barricades • traffic cones • portable visual alerting devices such as electric message signs • strobes • flares	Special facility structures, equipment and supplies for prolonged collective protection or sheltering CSEPP funds may not be used to fund public or private-sector first responder positions. OSHA Level A ensembles will not be funded, as the missions typically performed in this level of protective clothing are not consistent with CSEPP guidance.	

	Allowable costs include...	Unallowable costs include...	Cost apportionment items...
	Vehicles for decontamination and screening response (such as equipment trailers, trailer mounted decontamination systems, or prime movers for these trailers) may be allowable		
Public Outreach and Education (POE)	Costs, including contracts, for planning, equipment acquisition, and production and distribution of materials needed to inform and educate the public about CSEPP Costs for planning, equipment acquisition and/or leasing, installation, testing, operating a JIC facility		All-hazard information such as calendars, advertising promotional items and kiosks. Routine custodial, maintenance and utility costs for JICs
Training (TNG)	Training only for public and private sector responders whose agencies or organizations have a defined role in CSEPP as delineated in the jurisdiction's plan. This includes hospital employees whose facilities are designated CSEPP hospitals. Costs, including contracts, consistent with the current CSEPP Training Plan and necessary to maintain the proficiency of emergency services providers/responders and CSEPP staff Training for qualifying responders that meets other statutory or regulatory requirements applicable to those responders may be funded if the majority of learning objectives are also directly applicable to CSEPP and approval is obtained in advance. Training will be addressed and coordinated through the local site IPTs. Professional development training for CSEPP-funded employees where the training is directly relevant to the employee's CSEPP mission. Non-CSEPP –specific courses should be approved by the FEMA CSEPP Regional Program Manager on a case-by-case basis. CSEPP-related credentialing expenses for CSEPP-funded employees as approved by the FEMA CSEPP Regional Program Manager on a case-by-case basis.	Travel costs for training should be accounted for under Administration Training to meet statutory or regulatory requirements (including but not limited to OSHA PPE requirements, Hazardous Waste Operations (HAZWOPER), and OSHA employee emergency response requirements) for responders that do not have a defined role in CSEPP as delineated in the jurisdiction's plan. This includes hospital employees whose facilities are designated CSEPP hospitals but are not part of the CSEPP response plan. **Reallocation of training funds without prior approval**	Training with CSEPP-applicable content, where the majority of learning objectives are not directly applicable to CSEPP may be funded on a cost-apportionment basis with prior approval

V. Program Closeout Guidance

In accordance with the National Defense Authorization Act of 2008, assistance may be used to enhance and/or provide capabilities to respond to emergencies involving risks to the public health or safety from the storage of lethal chemical agents and munitions at disposal facilities until the earlier of the following:

- The date of the completion of all grants and cooperative agreements with respect to the installation or facility for purposes of this paragraph between the FEMA and the State and local governments concerned.

- The date that is 180 days after the local commander's treaty certification of the completion of the destruction of lethal chemical agents and munitions at the installation or facility.

This limitation applies only to the availability of new funding from FEMA to Grantees and Subgrantees after completion of the destruction of lethal chemical agents and munitions at the installation of facility, not to the expenditure of funds already awarded in open Cooperative Agreements. This limitation only applies to the destruction of lethal chemical agents and munitions at the installation or facility and does not consider destruction of hydrolysate or any contaminated materials or structures.

The 180 day period does not arbitrarily modify a previous awarded CA performance period. Performance period extensions will be negotiated in accordance with Part VI, Extension Policy for Cooperative Agreements.

Line items in the Cooperative Agreement or reallocations during this 180 day period must be sufficiently justified to FEMA to be considered for funding during the 180 day period. FEMA will not establish a specific list of what expenses that are allowable during the 180 day period are but will review line items for consideration.

VI. Indirect Cost Guidance

Grantees must submit a current approved signed cost allocation plan or indirect cost agreement for each Subgrantee requesting indirect costs as part of their application package to the DHS/FEMA Regional Office. The approved indirect cost agreement must be submitted with the Application for Federal Assistance (SF 424).

- CSEPPWebCA automatically calculates indirect costs.

- Subgrantees can use a cost allocation plan in lieu of an indirect cost agreement, as long as there is a written agreement signed by the proper jurisdictional authority stating the indirect cost parameters.

- A revised cost allocation plan or indirect cost agreement for each Subgrantee requesting indirect costs may not be submitted to adjust the rate during the performance period of a cooperative agreement. Information on indirect cost calculation is located in the Help feature of CSEPPWebCA. https://www.cseppwebca.net.

- Grantees and Subgrantees should be aware of and notify affected agencies and officials that the conclusion of CSEPP funding will end funding for indirect costs. Further, where indirect costs are based on specific types of costs, the availability of indirect costs may end sooner. For example, if indirect costs are based on equipment expenditures, and equipment expenditures cease with the end of preparedness, there will be no additional indirect cost funding available during the closeout period.

VII. Other Requirements

Life Cycle Cost Estimate (LCCE)

Jurisdictions should review and update the LCCE annually in coordination with the CSEPP Regional Program Manager. Cost estimates projected under the LCCE do not constitute an entitlement of funds to the State, Tribal, or local governments. However, the LCCE should be used as the basis for preparing future budget requests. Funding requirements identified in the LCCE must have been validated by the CSEPP Regional Program Manager and must be prioritized in the budget submission process. Cost estimates for validated requirements in the LCCE will be reduced if expenditures are consistently lower than projected estimates.

VIII. Insufficient Appropriations

Once all budget requests have been received, requested amounts will be totaled and the aggregate amount compared with available appropriated funding. If there is a shortfall between the total requested amount and available funds, DHS/FEMA will inform each State of its anticipated allocation of available funds. The State government will then be asked to prioritize its budget requests to remain within that anticipated amount. In prioritizing its requested budget items, the State should give preference to items needed to fund the most critical tasks.

IX. Application Review Information

Review Process

The Grantee and Subgrantee negotiates the funding requests with the CSEPP Regional Program Manager, using the LCCE as a guide. In reviewing the funding requests, the composition and scope of each of the Benchmarks will be governed by the principle of "functional equivalency" (i.e. it is not necessary to provide every jurisdiction with identical assets, as long as their basic emergency management capabilities meet CSEPP guidance).

The Grantee prepares the cooperative agreement application in accordance with the specific instructions in Appendix A. A printed copy of the complete and signed cooperative agreement application is then submitted by the Grantee to the CSEPP Regional Program Manager. The Regional Assistance Officer and the CSEPP Regional Program Manager will review the application and, if necessary, request any omitted information from the Grantee. After the completion of this review, the application (including Regional funding recommendations) will be forwarded by the FEMA Region through CSEPPWebCA to DHS/FEMA HQ for final approval.

Once all budget requests have been received, requested amounts will be totaled and the aggregate amount compared with available appropriated funding. If there is a shortfall between the total requested amount and available funds, DHS/FEMA will inform each State government of its anticipated allocation of available funds. The State government will then be asked to prioritize its budget requests to remain within that anticipated amount. In prioritizing its requested budget items, the State government should give preference to items needed to fund the most critical tasks.

Review and Selection Process
Not applicable.

Anticipated Announcement and Award Dates
Approved Cooperative Agreement awards are anticipated on or after October 1 of each fiscal year.

X.   **Post-Selection and Pre-Award Guidelines**

Notice of Award
Upon receipt of appropriated off-post funding from the Army and approval of SF 132 Apportionment Authority from the OMB, DHS/FEMA Program Office will provide the approved funding to each Regional Office.

The FEMA Regional Offices will provide an award package to the Grantee. Award packages will include an award letter, FEMA Form 76-10A, and Articles of Agreement (Appendix A). The FEMA Form 76-10A must be signed by the Grantee and returned to FEMA before funds can be obligated.

Post Award
Reporting requirements must be met throughout the life of each open Cooperative Agreement. Any reports or documents prepared as a result of this cooperative agreement shall be in compliance with Federal "plain English" policies, directives, etc., http://www.plainlanguage.gov.

Federal Financial Report {XE "Financial Status Report (FSR)"} (FFR)–required quarterly
Obligations and expenditures must be reported on a quarterly basis through the FFR (SF-425),which replaced the SF-269 and SF-272, and is due within 30 days of the end of each calendar quarter (e.g., for the quarter ending March 31, the FFR is due no later than April 30). A report must be submitted for every quarter of the period of performance, unless a waiver is granted. If there is no activity during a calendar quarter, the Grantee must transmit a performance report noting the inactivity. Future awards and

fund drawdowns may be withheld if these reports are delinquent. The final FFR is due 90 days after the end date of the performance period.

FFRs must be filed according to the schedule below:

- FFRs must be filed electronically through CSEPPWebCA

Reporting periods and due dates:

- October 1–December 31; Due January 30
- January 1–March 31; Due April 30
- April 1–June 30; Due July 30
- July 1–September 30; Due October 30

Revisions of Program Narratives and Budget

Any major change in project scope or funding amount requires a formal amendment to the cooperative agreement. Formal amendments require the signing of the FEMA Form 76-10A. The Regional Assistance Officer, in coordination with the CSEPP Regional Program Manager, approves or denies the request for change.

Budget Changes

Grantees shall obtain prior approval from DHS/FEMA whenever any of the following changes are anticipated:

- Any revision that would result in the need for additional funding.
- In accordance with 44 CFR, 13.30, Changes, cumulative transfers among direct cost categories, or, if applicable, among separately budgeted programs, projects, functions, or activities which exceed or are expected to exceed 10 percent of the current total approved budget.
- Transfer of funds allotted for training.

Only DHS/FEMA HQ can adjust the award amount in CSEPPWebCA for the above changes. Therefore, after the initial award is made, these budget changes must be forwarded to DHS/FEMA HQ through the CSEPP Regional Program Manager.

Programmatic Changes

Grantees must obtain prior written approval from the CSEPP Regional Program Manager and the Regional Assistance Officer whenever any of the following actions are anticipated:

- Any revision to the scope or objectives in the program narrative (regardless of whether there is an associated budget revision requiring prior approval or not).
- Need to extend the period of performance.
- Changes in key personnel or staff in cases where specified in a cooperative agreement.

- Subgranting, contracting out, or otherwise obtaining the services of a third party to perform activities which are central to the purposes of the award. This approval requirement does not apply to the procurement of equipment, supplies, and general support services.

Revision of Budget Under the 10 Percent Rule
In accordance with 44 CFR, Section 13.30 Changes, cumulative transfers among direct cost categories, or, if applicable, among separately budgeted programs, projects, functions, or activities which do not exceed ten percent of the current total approved budget may be made by the Grantee through CSEPPWebCA with notification to DHS/FEMA Region and HQ.

Reporting
CSEPPWebCA is used for both financial and performance reporting. A separate performance report is required for each funded Benchmark within the CA.

Extension Policy for Cooperative Agreements
DHS/FEMA's obligation of appropriated funds and their use by Grantees and Subgrantees are governed by established principles of Federal Appropriations Law. Consistent with that Law, this policy establishes a standard on award considerations concerning funding amounts and on the propriety of Grantee use of DHS/FEMA funds beyond the period for which they were originally awarded.

Descriptions:
- Period of availability (Appropriations Period):
  - Funds that are appropriated by Congress stipulate the period during which they are available for obligation.
  - Funds are available for obligation to the Grantee during the entire fiscal year(s) for which they are appropriated.
  - No reallocation or change in scope can be made to the Cooperative Agreement after the expiration of the appropriation.
- Period of performance:
  - The period of time shown in the Agreement Articles during which the Grantee is expected to perform the activities and obligate the funds included in the approved cooperative agreement.
  - A Grantee may not obligate CSEPP funds after the expiration of the specified period of performance unless that period is extended by DHS/FEMA Regional Office.
  - The Grantee has up to 90 days following the expiration of the period of performance to liquidate valid obligations made during the performance period.
- Bona Fide Need Rule is a principle that applies to DHS/FEMA's obligation of appropriated funds:

- DHS/FEMA may not obligate funds in a current period for unknown needs or for the needs of a future period.
  - Funds are awarded with the expectation that they will be used by the Grantee during the current period of performance.
  - Unliquidated obligations are valid obligations incurred by the Grantee during the stated period of performance for which payment has not occurred.
  - Unobligated balances are that portion of the funds that have not been obligated by the Grantee. They are determined by deducting the cumulative obligations from the cumulative funds authorized.

Extensions:
  - A Grantee may not obligate CSEPP funds after the expiration of the specified period of performance unless that period is extended by the DHS/FEMA Regional Assistance Officer.
  - A Grantee may make formal written request, not later than 60 days prior to expiration of the period of performance, for authority to extend the period of performance and/or carry some or all of the unobligated funds forward during the extended period to complete the approved cooperative agreement projects. The request for an extension must provide adequate justification for the action requested as follows:
    - Reason for delay:
      - Current status of the activity/activities;
      - Approved period of performance termination date and new project completion date;
      - Remaining available federal funds;
      - Budget outlining how remaining Federal funds will be expended;
      - Plan for completion including milestones and timeframes for achieving each milestone and the position/person responsible for implementing the plan for completion; and
      - Certification that the activity/activities will be completed within the extended period of performance without any modification to the original Statement of Work approved by FEMA.
  - A Grantee must have submitted all required financial status reports and performance reports, before the DHS/FEMA Regional Assistance Officer will process a request for extension.
  - The Regional Assistance Officer and the CSEPP Regional Program Manager will analyze the Grantee's justification and make the determination to extend the performance period.
  - If DHS/FEMA Regional Office is still reviewing the request at the end of the performance period and before the determination has been made, no further

activity should be undertaken until written notification is received from the DHS/FEMA Regional Assistance Officer.

- The Grantee/Subgrantees may continue to liquidate obligated funds.
- The DHS/FEMA Regional Office will not initiate closeout of the cooperative agreement while a decision is pending.

- One extension of the initial performance period of a cooperative agreement can be made by the Regional Assistance Officer in coordination with CSEPP Regional Program Manager; subsequent extensions must be approved by DHS/FEMA HQ.

- Performance periods may be extended even if no funds remain available for obligation in order to complete cooperative agreement management activities.

Inventory Records
In accordance with 44 CFR Subsection 13.32, Equipment, the Grantee will complete a physical inventory of all equipment and the results reconciled with the property records at least once every two years. Upon request, these inventory records shall be provided to DHS/FEMA. In addition, Grantees are invited to upload their inventory records into CSEPPWebCA as supporting documentation.

1. **Financial and Compliance Audit Report.** Recipients that expend $500,000 or more of Federal funds during their fiscal year are required to submit an organization-wide financial and compliance audit report. The audit must be performed in accordance with GAO's Government Auditing Standards, located at http://www.gao.gov/govaud/ybk01.htm, and OMB Circular A-133, Audits of States, Local Governments, and Non-Profit Organizations, located at http://www.whitehouse.gov/sites/default/files/omb/assets/a133/a133_revised_2007.pdf. Audit reports are currently due to the Federal Audit Clearinghouse no later than nine months after the end of the recipient's fiscal year. In addition, the Secretary of Homeland Security and the Comptroller General of the United States shall have access to any books, documents, and records of recipients of FY 2013 assistance for audit and examination purposes, provided that, in the opinion of the Secretary or the Comptroller, these documents are related to the receipt or use of such assistance. The Grantee will also give the sponsoring agency or the Comptroller, through any authorized representative, access to, and the right to examine all records, books, papers or documents related to the cooperative agreement.

   Grantees that expend less than $500,000 are exempt from A-133 Federal audit requirements for that year, but records must be available for review or audit by appropriate officials of DHS/FEMA, pass-through entity and the GAO.

   The State shall require that Subgrantees comply with the audit requirements set forth in OMB Circular A-133. Recipients are responsible for ensuring that sub-recipient audit reports are received and for resolving any audit findings.

2. **Monitoring.** Cooperative agreement recipients will be monitored periodically by FEMA staff, both programmatically and financially, to ensure that the project goals, objectives, performance requirements, timelines, milestone completion, budgets, and other related program criteria are being met.

   Monitoring will be accomplished through a combination of desk-based reviews and on-site monitoring visits. Monitoring will involve the review and analysis of the financial, programmatic, performance and administrative issues relative to each program and will identify areas where technical assistance and other support may be needed.

   The recipient is responsible for monitoring award activities, to include sub-awards, to provide reasonable assurance that the Federal award is administered in compliance with requirements. Responsibilities include the accounting of receipts and expenditures, cash management, maintaining of adequate financial records, and refunding expenditures disallowed by audits.

3. **Cooperative Agreement Close-Out Process.** This is the phase during which the Regional Assistance Officer and the CSEPP Regional Program Manager determines that all administrative and programmatic actions have been completed by the Grantee and DHS/FEMA. In accordance with 44 CFR 13.50, after-the-grant requirements involve closing out the assistance agreement, including adjustment of the award amount and the amount of cash paid the Grantee.

   - Not later than 60 days prior to the expiration of the performance period, the Regional Assistance Officer notifies the Grantee that the assistance agreement will end. This notification also includes the actions to be accomplished by Grantee in fulfillment of their responsibilities.

   - Actions that must precede closeout are receipt of all required reports, disposition or recovery of all Federal property, and adjustment of the award amount and the amount of Federal cash paid the Grantee.

   - Unobligated balances are that portion of the funds that have not been obligated by the Grantee. They are determined by deducting the cumulative obligations from the cumulative funds authorized. If any unobligated balance remains at the end of the period of performance, these funds are no longer available to DHS/FEMA or the Grantee and are subject to being returned to the U.S. Treasury.

   - Unliquidated obligations are valid obligations incurred by the Grantee during the stated period of performance for which payment has not occurred. If such obligations are not liquidated by the end of the closeout period, no further CSEPP reimbursement will be available.

- Equipment inventories and requests for disposition of equipment should be prepared and submitted to DHS/FEMA Region in accordance with the provisions of 44 CFR Part 13. Equipment that will continue to be used and maintained in the CSEP Program shall be noted on the disposition request. Note that separate requirements exist for property provided by federal agencies.

- CSEPPWebCA should be used to create the final SF 425 and the final quarterly performance report, however, a copy of your SF 425 should be uploaded in CSEPPWebCA. Other closeout documents will be uploaded in the CSEPPWebCA filing cabinet by the Regional Assistance Officer.

- After the 90-day closeout period the Grantee must submit a final FFR and final progress report detailing all accomplishments throughout the period of performance. The official file will be reviewed and missing items needed to close out will be identified. The Grantee will be notified of all missing items, outstanding reports, and requirements needed to complete closeout.

- After closeout requirements have been satisfied, the Regional Assistance Officer sends the Closeout Satisfaction Letter to the Grantee.

- The Grantee will maintain the cooperative agreement records for three years from the date of the final FFR.

- The Grantee is responsible for returning any funds that have been drawn down but remain as unliquidated on Grantee financial records.

- If funds need to be returned to FEMA after the completion of grant closeout (e.g., as a result of a subsequent audit), the FEMA Regional Office will notify the FEMA HQ CSEPP office of any adjustments to the final approved expenditures.

- Grantees are encouraged to complete the closeout of prior year Cooperative Agreements before to the end of the performance period of that CA.

- Upon completion of grant closeout, access to CSEPPWebCA for Grantees and Subgrantees will cease. A CD for the Grantee and/or Subgrantee can be produced and made available upon request from your Regional POC. Any subsequent requirements for access to the system should be directed to the CSEPPWebCA Help Desk at (888) 784-6610.

- CSEPPWebCA Help contains guidance on how to initiate and complete closeout.

XI. DHS/FEMA Contact Information

Contact and Resource Information
CSEPP is administered at FEMA Headquarters in partnership with the CSEPP Regional Offices.

1. **Program Office Contact.**
   FEMA Headquarters, CSEPP Program Office
   Terrence Hobbs, Branch Chief, (703) 605-1379

2. **FEMA Regions.** FEMA Regions will provide fiscal support, including pre- and post-award administration, monitoring and technical assistance to the cooperative agreement programs included in this solicitation. For a list of contacts, please go to:
   https://www.cseppportal.net/secure/portal/contacts/Lists/CSSEPP%20Headq uarters/AllItems.aspx.

   Region IV
   Robert Madden, CSEPP Program Manager, (770) 220-5478
   Sandra McNease, Assistance Officer, (229) 225-4636

   Region VIII
   Douglas Becvar, CSEPP Program Manager, (303) 235-4997
   Crystal Lehnhardt, Assistance Officer, (303) 235-4858

XII.   Other Critical Information

Presidential Policy Directive 8: National Preparedness

On March 30, 2011, the President released Presidential Policy Directive 8 (PPD-8), which focuses on strengthening the security and resilience of the United States through systematic preparation for the threats that pose the greatest risk to the security of the Nation, including acts of terrorism, cyber-attacks, pandemics, and catastrophic natural disasters. As defined in PPD-8, national preparedness refers to *"the actions taken to plan, organize, equip, train and exercise to build and sustain the capabilities necessary to prevent, protect against, mitigate the effects of, respond to, and recover from those threats that pose the greatest risk to the security of the Nation."* National preparedness is the shared responsibility of all levels of government, the private and nonprofit sectors, and individual citizens. PPD-8 objective is to facilitate an integrated, all-of-Nation, capabilities-based approach to preparedness.

PPD-8 required the development of a National Preparedness Goal (NPG). The NPG sets the vision for preparedness nationwide and identifies core capabilities essential for the execution of each of the five mission areas: prevention, protection, mitigation, response, and recovery. The NPG's core capabilities are the distinct critical elements necessary for our success in achieving national preparedness. The core capabilities represent an evolution from the Target Capabilities List (TCL). The transition from TCLs to core capabilities expands the focus to include mitigation and allows greater focus on prevention and protection activities.

PPD-8 also provided for the development of a National Preparedness System (NPS). The NPS is to be an integrated set of guidance, programs, and processes that can be implemented and measured at all levels of government, thereby enabling the Nation to achieve the Goal. The System will be based on a consistent methodology for assessing the threats and hazards facing a given jurisdiction. The findings of such assessments should then drive planning factors and all other components of the preparedness cycle including resource requirements, existing capabilities and capability gaps, driving investments to close those gaps, making and validating improvements in capabilities through training and exercising, and continually assessing progress.

As part of building and sustaining preparedness, the Directive calls for providing Federal financial assistance to support a comprehensive campaign to build and sustain national preparedness, including public outreach and community-based and private-sector programs to enhance national resilience.

The full text of PPD-8 and NPG can be found at http://www.dhs.gov/xabout/laws/gc_1215444247124.shtm and http://www.fema.gov/pdf/prepared/npg.pdf, respectively.

Emergency Management Assistance Compact (EMAC) Membership
In support of the National Preparedness Goal, Cooperative Agreement recipients must belong to member States of EMAC.

National Incident Management System (NIMS) Implementation
In accordance with Homeland Security Presidential Directive (HSPD)-5, *Management of Domestic Incidents*, the adoption of NIMS is a requirement to receive Federal preparedness assistance, through grants, contracts, and other activities.

The Grantee is responsible for determining if Subgrantees have demonstrated sufficient progress in NIMS implementation prior to disbursing awards.

FEMA has developed the *NIMS Guideline for Credentialing of Personnel* to describe national credentialing standards and to provide written guidance regarding the use of those standards. This guideline describes credentialing and typing processes and identifies tools which Federal Emergency Response Officials (FERO) and emergency managers at all levels of government may use both routinely and to facilitate multijurisdictional coordinated responses.

Emergency Operations Plans
Grantees must update emergency operations plans at least once every two years in accordance with CPG101, November 2010.

Exercises
Exercises conducted with CSEPP funding support should be managed and executed in accordance with the Exercise Policy and Guidance for Chemical Stockpile Emergency Preparedness Program Exercise which integrates the Homeland Security Exercise and Evaluation Program (HSEEP). Exercise Policy and Guidance for Chemical Stockpile Emergency Preparedness Program Exercise is located at http://orise.orau.gov/csepp/resources/documents/training-management-guidance.pdf.

HSEEP Guidance for exercise design, development, conduct, evaluation, and improvement planning is located at https://hseep.dhs.gov.

XIII. How to Apply

Application Instructions

The CSEPP CA is managed through a web application called CSEPPWebCA https://www.cseppwebca.net. CSEPPWebCA creates the required narrative statements, work plans, funding requests, and the financial forms that meet the requirements of the Office of Management and Budget (OMB) Circular A-102, Grants and Cooperative Agreements with State and local governments http://www.whitehouse.gov/omb/circulars_a102/. The required documents will be automatically produced and submitted through this process. This software produces the following documents:

1. SF 424, Application for Federal Assistance (attach Indirect Cost Agreement if reimbursements for indirect costs are requested).

2. SF 425, Federal Financial Report.

3. Program Narrative Statement.

4. FEMA Form 20-16, Summary Sheet for Assurances Parts 1, 2, 3 & 4 and Certifications.

5. Work Plans for all CSEPP funded personnel.

6. Request for Funding Worksheets.

Subgrantees are required to prepare a six-part (or seven-parts if construction is involved) CSEPP CA Pre-Award Application. The State consolidates all Subgrantee submissions.

SF 424C (Budget Information-Construction) and SF 424D (Standard Assurances-Construction) must be submitted on construction projects. These forms are available in a fillable PDF form available from OMB, http://www.usa-federal-forms.com/sf.html.

A COMPLETE CA APPLICATION PACKAGE MUST BE PRINTED, SIGNED, AND SUBMITTED TO YOUR REGIONAL CSEPP PROGRAM MANAGER.

The program title listed in the CFDA is "Chemical Stockpile Emergency Preparedness Program (CSEPP)." The CFDA number is 97.040.

1. Dun and Bradstreet Data Universal Numbering System (DUNS) number. The Grantee must provide a DUNS number with their application. This number is a required field within https://www.cseppwebca.net/Login.aspx?p=1. Organizations should verify that they have a DUNS number, or take the steps necessary to obtain one, as soon as possible. Grantees can receive a DUNS number or make modifications to their existing DUNS record at no cost by calling the dedicated toll-free DUNS Number request line at (866) 705-5711 or visit https://fedgov.dnb.com/webform.

2. CCR Validation. Eligible Grantees can confirm Central Contract Registration (CCR) registration at http://www.ccr.gov.

3. Program Specific Narrative and Work Plan Narrative

The program narrative for non-construction programs provides a brief description of the objective, need, approach, results or benefits expected, and the geographical location of the project and the benefits expected to be obtained from the assistance as outlined in OMB Circular A-102. In the CSEPP CA, objective and need correlate to goal; approach correlates to task description; results or benefits expected correlate to expected outcomes and geographical location correlates to the State or local government.

A program narrative statement must be prepared for each applicable CSEPP National Benchmark (CNB). Guidance for preparing narratives in the CA is found in the Help Pre-Award Section in the CSEPPWebCA web site. A suggested template for CNB program narratives can be found on the CSEPP Portal https://www.csepportal.net/secure/portal/Benchmarks/administrative/Cooperative Agreements/SampleProgramNarratives.doc.

Narratives should be constructed in accordance with the following guidance from OMB Circular A-102, paragraph (5) (a):

Objective (Goal)

- Pinpoint any relevant physical, economic, social, financial, institutional, or other problems requiring a solution.

- Demonstrate the need for assistance and state the principle and subordinate objectives of the project. Supporting documentation or other testimonies from concerned interests other than the Grantee may be used. Any relevant data based on planning studies should be included or footnoted.

Approach (Plan of Action)

- Outline a plan of action pertaining to the scope and detail of how the proposed work will be accomplished for each cooperative agreement program.

- Cite factors which might accelerate or decelerate the work and your reason for taking this approach as opposed to others.

- Describe any unusual features of the program such as design or technological innovations, reductions in cost or time, or extraordinary social and community involvement.

- Provide projections of the accomplishments to be achieved through the cooperative agreement. List a schedule, in chronological order, of accomplishments.

- Identify the kinds of data to be collected and maintained and discuss the criteria to be used to evaluate the results and successes of the project.

- Explain the methodology that will be used to determine if the needs identified and discussed are being met and if the results and benefits identified are being achieved.
- List each organization, consultant, or other key individuals who will work on the project along with a short description of the nature of their effort or contribution.

Results or Benefits Expected

- Identify results and benefits to be derived with respect to the emergency preparedness capabilities of the Grantee/Subgrantee.

Geographic Location

- Complete Item 12 in the Standard Form 424 "Areas Affected by Project (cities, counties, States, etc.).

Work Plans

- Each CSEPP employee must submit an annual work plan using CSEPPWebCA. In developing Work Plans, the following must be considered:
- CSEPP funded positions are restricted in their availability to perform non-CSEPP activities and must work full-time on CSEPP.
- CSEPP funded employees can respond and support emergencies or disasters within their jurisdictions for a period of up to two weeks.
- For Federally-declared disasters, employees' time should be charged directly to the disaster code.
- If a position is partially funded by CSEPP, the Grantee/Subgrantee must ensure that the individual's time performing CSEPP-related work is proportional to the percentage paid by CSEPP.
- Identify tasks to be performed by the individual staffing each fully or partially CSEPP-funded position.
- Describe tasks in measureable terms.
- Identify expected results of task performance.
- Identify schedules for performance of tasks.
- If there is no other agreement in place, FEMA will offer to extend funding for preparedness-focused activities through the end of the quarter in which demilitarization ends (rather than just up to the exact date that demilitarization operations end). After that point, all funded CSEPP personnel must have clearly defined closeout roles in their annual work plans.
- Sample Work Plans are available on the CSEPP Portal under the Administration Benchmark section. Select the following links to access the sample county Work Plans
  https://www.cseppportal.net/secure/portal/Benchmarks/administrative/Cooperativ

e%20Agreements/Workplans/County_WorkPlan.doc or sample State Work Plans https://www.cseppportal.net/secure/portal/Benchmarks/administrative/Cooperativ e%20Agreements/Workplans/State_WorkPlan.doc.

XIV.   Applications and Submission Information

The State government is invited to submit a pre-award application. This invitation contains the guidance package for preparing a CSEPP Cooperative Agreement Pre-Award Application.

Region IV
National Preparedness Division/CSEPP Section
3003 Chamblee-Tucker Road
Atlanta, GA 30341
(770) 220-5478

Region VIII
National Preparedness Division/CSEPP Section
Denver Federal Center
Bldg. 710
Box 25267
Denver, CO 80225-0267
(303) 235-4997

FEMA Headquarters
Department of Homeland Security
Federal Emergency Management Agency
Protection and National Preparedness
Technological Hazards Division
Chemical Stockpile Emergency Preparedness Program
1800 South Bell Street
Crystal City, Virginia 20598-3025
(703) 605-1379

Website Address
Online Application Process
https://www.cseppwebca.net/Login.aspx?p=1

New users need to contact the help desk for username and password assistance.
CSEPPWebCA Help Desk (888) 784-6610 or helpdesk@cseppwebca.net

This page intentionally left blank.

Appendix A: Articles of Agreement

CSEPP COOPERATIVE AGREEMENT ARTICLES

Grantee:_____

Agreement Number:_____ Amendment Number:_____

Designated Agency:_____

Performance Period Using O&M Funds:_____

Period of Federal Obligational Availability, When Using O&M Funds,

Ends On:_____

Performance Period Using Procurement Funds: _____

Period of Federal Obligational Availability, When Using Procurement Funds, Ends

On:_____

ARTICLE I. AUTHORIZATION. The United States of America through the Regional Administrator, Department of Homeland Security/Federal Emergency Management Agency (DHS/FEMA) or his delegate, agrees to grant to the State through its designated agency named above (hereinafter referred to as "the Grantee") funds in the amount specified on the FEMA Form 76-10A, Obligating Document for Award/Amendment, for the Federal share authorized under the Department of Defense Authorization Act of 1996, Public Law 99-145; Department of Defense Appropriation Act, 2000 (PL 106-79, October 25, 1999); Memorandum of Understanding between DHS/FEMA and the Army, dated March 2004; during the period specified above and in accordance with the approved cooperative agreement and terms and conditions set out in this document and the cooperative agreement application identified below and made a part hereof by reference. By acceptance of the funds granted, the Grantee agrees to abide by the terms and conditions of the cooperative agreement as set forth in these articles.

ARTICLE II. EFFECTIVE DATE. This cooperative agreement takes effect at the beginning of the Federal fiscal year (October 1).

ARTICLE III. PURPOSE. This cooperative agreement is for the administration and oversight of an approved CSEPP State and local governments. Cooperative agreement funds shall not be used for other purposes. As a condition of the cooperative agreement, the CSEPP State and local governments shall implement the cooperative agreement as approved by the Regional Administrator, DHS/FEMA.

ARTICLE IV. GENERAL PROVISIONS. The following are hereby incorporated into this agreement by reference:

44 CFR		Emergency Management and Assistance Regulations
44 CFR	Part 7	Nondiscrimination in Federally-Assisted Programs (DHS/FEMA)
44 CFR	Part 10	Environmental Considerations
44 CFR	Part 13	Uniform administrative requirements for grants and cooperative agreements to State, Tribal and Local
44 CFR	Part 17	Government wide debarment and suspension (non-procurement) and government wide requirements for drug-free workplace (grants)
44 CFR	Part 18	Restrictions on lobbying
44 CFR		SUBCHAPTER C–Fire Prevention and Control
44 CFR		SUBCHAPTER E–Preparedness
31 CFR § 205.6		Funding techniques
48 CFR	Part 31	Federal Acquisitions Regulations (FAR), Contracts with Commercial Organizations
PL101-391		Hotel and Motel Fire Safety Act of 1990
P.L. 101-336		The Americans With Disabilities Act
40 USC § 276a		The Davis-Bacon Act of 1931
E.O. 12372		Intergovernmental Reviews of the DHS/FEMA Programs and Activities
OMB Circular A-21		Cost Principles for Educational Institutions
OMB Circular A-87		Cost Principles for State, Local, and Indian Tribal Governments

OMB Circular A-102	Grants and Cooperative Agreements with State and Local Governments
OMB Circular A-110	Uniform Administrative Requirements for Grants and Agreements with Institutions of Higher Education, Hospitals, and Other Non-Profit Organizations
OMB Circular A-122	Cost Principles for Nonprofit Organizations
OMB Circular A-129	Policies for Federal Credit Programs and Non-Tax Receivables
OMB Circular A-133	Audits of States, Local Governments, and Non-Profit Organizations
PPD-8	Presidential Policy Directive 8: National Preparedness
HSPD-5	Homeland Security Presidential Directive, Management of Domestic Incident (NIMS)
Guidance	Guidance for Preparing and Managing the Chemical Stockpile Emergency Preparedness Program (CSEPP) Cooperative Agreement (CA) Application for Fiscal Year 2013

ARTICLE V. REQUEST FOR ADVANCE/REIMBURSEMENT. The Recipient shall be paid in advance using the HHS SMARTLINK System, provided it maintains or demonstrates the willingness and ability to maintain procedures to minimize the time elapsing between the transfer of the funds and their disbursement by the Recipient. When these requirements are not met, the Recipient will be required to use the reimbursement method as the preferred funding method.

ARTICLE VI. SPECIFIC TERMS AND CONDITIONS. The specific terms and conditions of this agreement are as follows:

1. The recipients of CSEPP funding must use CSEPPWebCA for preparing, managing, and quarterly reporting on their CSEPP Cooperative Agreement.

2. States and local governments will continue to meet the minimum requirements for NIMS.

3. The tasks approved in CSEPPWebCA are to be undertaken by the Grantee utilizing the funds identified on FEMA Form 76-10A.

4. For jurisdictions requesting indirect costs, an approved indirect cost agreement (IDC) or an approved cost allocation plan must be submitted at the beginning of each Federal Fiscal Year as an attachment to the State's Request for Federal Assistance. Once the indirect cost agreement or cost

allocation plan is filed, there will be no adjustments to the rate for the duration of the cooperative agreement.

5. The funds for the cooperative agreement shall only be used to cover allowable costs that are incurred during the agreement period. In addition, valid obligations incurred before the end of the agreement period for purchased services, equipment, and supplies specifically identified in the approved application shall be considered allowable cooperative agreement period costs to the extent of actual subsequent expenditures. If obligations are included in the claimed cooperative agreement costs, adequate records shall be maintained to disclose fully the date and amount incurred and the date and amount of subsequent payment. Obligations claimed in one cooperative agreement period shall be excluded from expenditures claimed in prior or subsequent periods.

6. The Grantee shall follow prior approval requirements found in 44 CFR Part 13.30. For non-construction cooperative agreements, transfers of funds between total direct cost categories in the approved budget shall receive the prior approval of DHS/FEMA when such transfers exceed 10 percent of the total budget.

7. No transfer of funds to agencies other than those identified in the approved cooperative agreement application shall be made without prior approval of DHS/FEMA.

8. The Grantee shall submit financial reports 30 days after the end of each quarter. Reporting dates are: January 30, April 30, July 30, and October 30. Final financial reports are due 90 days after the close of the cooperative agreement. Copies of the FFR (SF 425) are to be submitted to the DHS/FEMA Regional Office, Attn: Assistance Officer.

9. The Grantee shall submit performance reports for each funded CSEPP National Benchmark 30 days after the end of each quarter. Reporting dates are: January 30, April 30, July 30, and October 30. The final performance report is due 90 days after the close of the Cooperative Agreement. Copies of the performance report are to be submitted to the DHS/FEMA Regional Office, ATTN: Assistance Officer.

10. The Grantee shall transfer to DHS/FEMA the appropriate share, based on the Federal support percentage, of any refund, rebate, credit or other amounts arising from the performance of this agreement, along with accrued interest, if any. The Grantee shall take necessary action to effect prompt collection of all monies due or which may become due and to cooperate with DHS/FEMA in any claim or suit in connection with amounts due. When reporting CSEPP Program Income the amount is to be deducted from total allowable costs to determine the net allowable costs committed to the cooperative agreement by DHS/FEMA and the Grantee. The program income shall be used for the purposes and under conditions for the cooperative agreement. (44 CFR 13.25 (g) (1). Deductive Method).

11. Prior to the start of any construction activity, the Grantee shall ensure that all applicable Federal, State or Tribal government and local permits and clearances are obtained to include environmental planning and historic preservation compliance.

12. The Grantee may copyright any original work developed in the course of or under the agreement. DHS/FEMA reserves a royalty-free, nonexclusive and irrevocable right to reproduce, publish or otherwise use, and to authorize others to use, the work for government purposes. Any publication resulting from work performed under this agreement shall include an acknowledgement of DHS/FEMA financial support and a statement that the publication does not necessarily reflect DHS/FEMA views.

13. No subsequent cooperative agreements, monetary increase amendments, or time extension amendments will be approved unless all overdue financial or performance reports have been submitted by the recipient to the appropriate Regional Office. The Grantee agrees, by accepting the funds in the aforementioned cooperative agreement from DHS/FEMA, to comply with all the provisions of 44 CFR Subsection 13.32, Equipment, which states "a physical inventory must be taken and the results reconciled with the property records at least once every two years." Upon request, these inventory records shall be provided to DHS/FEMA.

14. CSEPP funds may not be used to fund other programs required by other laws for existing needs. CSEPP funds may not be used to supplant other forms of emergency management funding. An example of the inappropriate use of CSEPP funds would be charging all or a substantial portion of personnel costs or Emergency Operations Center (EOC) costs to CSEPP when they should be and/or were previously part of the ongoing emergency management budget.

15. For cost allocation projects, CSEPP is not necessarily responsible for any or all of the maintenance or replacement costs. Although, CSEPP may have paid for certain equipment in its entirety, if that equipment is being used for non-CSEPP activities, CSEPP is only obligated to pay the portion of Operations and Maintenance (O&M) costs commensurate to its CSEPP use.

16. CSEPP funds may not be commingled with other, non-CSEPP funds. In keeping with the intent of the congressional appropriations, and to assure proper programmatic accountability, CSEPP funds must at all times remain separate and apart from any other DHS/FEMA or non-DHS/FEMA funding sources. Funds from each awarded CA must remain separate, distinct and cannot be commingled with funding from other CAs.

17. CSEPP personnel positions fully funded by CSEPP are restricted in their availability to perform non-CSEPP activities and must work full time on CSEPP. CSEPP funded employees can respond and support emergencies or disasters within their jurisdictions for a period of up to two weeks. When a position is only partially funded by the CSEPP, this should be reflected in the work plan and the supervisor is responsible and accountable for ensuring that

the individual's time performing for CSEPP is in direct proportion to the percent paid by the CSEPP.

18. If a recipient estimates that it will have unobligated funds remaining after the end of the performance period, the recipient should report this to the DHS/FEMA Regional Office at the earliest possible time and ask for disposition instructions.

19. Grantees will participate annually in the national CSEPP exercise program. The States will use the web-based Homeland Security Exercise and Evaluation Program (HSEEP) Corrective Action Program (CAP) to track all Findings Requiring Corrective Actions (FRCAs). Users should use existing DHS/CAP guidance to implement this program.

20. To assist in fully integrating HSEEP into the CSEPP exercise program, all CSEPP funded employees who evaluate CSEPP exercises must complete the HSEEP Independent Study Courses; IS120a, An Orientation to Community Disaster Exercises; IS130, Exercise Evaluation and Improvement Planning. All CSEPP funded employees who plan exercises must complete IS139, Exercise Design; and L146 Homeland Security Exercise and Evaluation Program (HSEEP) Training Course. A copy of the certificate should be forwarded to the State/Tribe CSEPP Program Manager by the end of the federal fiscal year.

ARTICLE VII. All Sub-recipients that follow OMB Circular No. A-110 must follow the audit requirements of OMB Circular No. A-133 Revised.

ARTICLE VIII. DHS/FEMA will conduct on-site monitoring visits to review both the program and financial progress of the Cooperative Agreement's activities. Technical assistance will be provided upon request. As a result of these on-site visits, DHS/FEMA will make recommendations to resolve any deficiencies.

Appendix B: Administrative and National Policy Requirements

All successful applicants for all DHS grant and cooperative agreements are required to comply with DHS Standard Administrative Terms and Conditions available at http://www.dhs.gov/xlibrary/assets/cfo-financial-management-policy-manual.pdf.

The recipient and any sub-recipient(s) must, in addition to the assurances made as part of the application, comply and require each of its subcontractors employed in the completion of the project to comply with all applicable statutes, regulations, executive orders, OMB Circulars, terms and condition of the award, and the approved application.

1. Standard Financial Requirements. The Grantee and any Subgrantee(s) shall comply with all applicable laws and regulations. A non-exclusive list of regulations commonly applicable to DHS/FEMA cooperative agreements are listed below:

   ## 1.1 Administrative Requirements.

   44 CFR Part 13, Uniform Administrative Requirements for Grants and Cooperative Agreements to State and Local Governments

   2 CFR Part 215, Uniform Administrative Requirements for Grants and Agreements with Institutions of Higher Education, Hospitals, and Other Non-Profit Organizations (formerly OMB Circular A-110)

   ## 1.2 Cost Principles.

   2 CFR Part 225, Cost Principles for State, Local, and Indian Tribal Governments (formerly OMB Circular A-87)

   2 CFR Part 220, Cost Principles for Educational Institutions (formerly OMB Circular A-21)

   2 CFR Part 230, Cost Principles for Non-Profit Organizations (formerly OMB Circular A-122)

   48 CFR 31.2, Federal Acquisitions Regulations (FAR), Contracts with Commercial Organizations

   ## 1.3 Audit Requirements

   OMB Circular A-133, Audits of States, Local Governments, and Non-Profit Organizations

   1.4 **Duplication of Benefits.** There may not be a duplication of any Federal assistance by governmental entities, per 2 CFR Part 225, Basic Guidelines Section C.3 (c), which states: Any cost allocable to a particular

Federal award or cost objective under the principles provided for in this authority may not be charged to other Federal awards to overcome fund deficiencies, to avoid restrictions imposed by law or terms of the Federal awards, or for other reasons. However, this prohibition would not preclude governmental units from shifting costs that are allowable under two or more awards in accordance with existing program agreements. Non-governmental entities are also subject to this prohibition per 2 CFR Parts 220 and 230 and 48 CFR 31.2.

2. Payment. DHS/FEMA uses the Direct Deposit/Electronic Funds Transfer (DD/EFT) method of payment to Recipients. To enroll in the DD/EFT, the Recipient must complete a Standard Form 1199A, Direct Deposit Form, found at http://www.ssa.gov/deposit/1199a.pdf.

   - FEMA utilizes the Department of Health and Human Services, Division of Payment Management, Payment Management System, SMARTLINK to transfer funds between FEMA and Grantees; or

   - The Recipient may be paid in advance, or reimbursed by completing the Standard Form (SF) 270, Request for Advance/Reimbursement. In order to download the Standard Form 270, the Recipient may use the following link: http://www.whitehouse.gov/sites/default/files/omb/grants/sf270.pdf.

   2.1 **Advance Payment.** In accordance with Treasury regulations at 31 CFR Part 205, the Recipient shall maintain procedures to minimize the time elapsing between the transfer of funds and the disbursement of said funds (See 44 CFR Part 13.21(i)) regarding payment of interest earned on advances. In order to request an advance, the Recipient must maintain or demonstrate the willingness and ability to maintain procedures to minimize the time elapsing between the transfer of funds from DHS/FEMA and expenditure and disbursement by the Recipient. When these requirements are not met, the Recipient will be required to be on a reimbursement-for-costs-incurred method.

   NOTE: FUNDS WILL NOT BE AUTOMATICALLY TRANSFERRED UPON ISSUANCE OF THE COOPERATIVE AGREEMENT. GRANTEES MUST SUBMIT A REQUEST FOR ADVANCE/REIMBURSEMENT (SF-270) IN ORDER FOR THE FUNDS TO BE TRANSFERRED TO THE GRANTEE'S ACCOUNT.

3. **Non-supplanting Requirement.** Cooperative agreement funds will be used to supplement existing funds, and will not replace (supplant) funds that have been appropriated for the same purpose. Grantees or Subgrantees may be required to supply documentation certifying that a reduction in non-Federal resources occurred for reasons other than the receipt or expected receipt of Federal funds.

Appendix B: Administrative and National Policy Requirements

4. **Administrative Requirements.**

   4.1 Freedom of Information Act (FOIA). FEMA recognizes that much of the information submitted in the course of applying for funding under this program or provided in the course of its cooperative agreement management activities may be considered law enforcement sensitive or otherwise important to national security interests. While this information under Federal control is subject to requests made pursuant to the Freedom of Information Act (FOIA), 5 U.S.C. §552, all determinations concerning the release of information of this nature are made on a case-by-case basis by the FEMA FOIA Office, and may likely fall within one or more of the available exemptions under the Act. The Grantee is encouraged to consult its own State and local laws and regulations regarding the release of information, which should be considered when reporting sensitive matters in the cooperative agreement application, needs assessment and strategic planning process. The Grantee should be familiar with the regulations governing Sensitive Security Information (49 CFR Part 1520), as it may provide additional protection to certain classes of homeland security information.

   4.2 Compliance with Federal civil rights laws and regulations. The grantee is required to comply with Federal civil rights laws and regulations. Specifically, the grantee is required to provide assurances as a condition for receipt of Federal funds that its programs and activities comply with the following:

   - Title VI of the Civil Rights Act of 1964, as amended, 42. U.S.C. §2000 et. seq. Provides that no person on the grounds of race, color, or national origin be excluded from participation in, be denied the benefits of, or be otherwise subjected to discrimination in any program or activity receiving Federal financial assistance. Title VI also extends protection to persons with Limited English Proficiency (LEP). (42 U.S.C. §2000d et seq.)

   - Title IX of the Education Amendments of 1972, as amended, 20 U.S.C. §1681 et. seq. Provides that no person, on the basis of sex, be excluded from participation in, be denied the benefits of, or be subject to discrimination under any education program or activity receiving Federal financial assistance.

   - Section 504 of the Rehabilitation Act of 1973, as amended, 29 U.S.C. §794 Provides that no otherwise qualified individual with a disability in the United States, shall, solely by reason of his or her disability, be excluded from the participation in, be denied the benefits of, or subject to discrimination in any program or activity receiving Federal financial assistance.

   - The Age Discrimination Act of 1975, as amended, 20 U.S.C. §6101 et. seq. Provides that no person in the United States shall, on the basis of

Appendix B: Administrative and National Policy Requirements

age, be excluded from participation in, be denied the benefits of, or be subject to discrimination under any program or activity receiving Federal financial assistance

Grantees must comply with all regulations, guidelines, and standards adopted under the above statutes. The grantee is also required to submit information, as required, to the DHS/FEMA Office for Civil Rights and Civil Liberties concerning its compliance with these laws and their implementing regulations.

4.3 Services to Limited English Proficient (LEP) persons. Recipients of FEMA financial assistance are required to comply with several Federal civil rights laws, including Title VI of the Civil Rights Act of 1964, as amended. These laws prohibit discrimination on the basis of race, color, religion, national origin, and sex in the delivery of services. National origin discrimination includes discrimination on the basis of limited English proficiency. To ensure compliance with Title VI, recipients are required to take reasonable steps to ensure that LEP persons have meaningful access to their programs. Meaningful access may entail providing language assistance services, including oral and written translation, where necessary. The grantee is encouraged to consider the need for language services for LEP persons served or encountered both in developing their proposals and budgets and in conducting their programs and activities. Reasonable costs associated with providing meaningful access for LEP individuals are considered allowable program costs. For additional information, see http://www.lep.gov.

4.4 Certifications and Assurances. Certifications and assurances regarding the following apply:

- Lobbying. 31 U.S.C. §1352, Limitation on use of appropriated funds to influence certain Federal contracting and financial transactions. – Prohibits the use of Federal funds in lobbying members and employees of Congress, as well as employees of Federal agencies, with respect to the award or amendment of any Federal grant, cooperative agreement, contract, or loan. FEMA and DHS have codified restrictions upon lobbying at 44 CFR Part 18 and 6 CFR Part 9. (Refer to form included in application package.)

- Drug-free Workplace Act, as amended, 41 U.S.C. §701 et seq. Requires the recipient to publish a statement about its drug-free workplace program and give a copy of the statement to each employee (including consultants and temporary personnel) who will be involved in award-supported activities at any site where these activities will be carried out. Also, place(s) where work is being performed under the award (i.e., street address, city, state and zip code) must be maintained on file. The recipient must notify the Grants Officer of any

Appendix B: Administrative and National Policy Requirements

employee convicted of a violation of a criminal drug statute that occurs in the workplace. For additional information, see 44 CFR Part 17.

- Debarment and Suspension. Executive Orders 12549 and 12689 provide protection from fraud, waste, and abuse by debarring or suspending those persons that deal in an irresponsible manner with the Federal government. The recipient must certify that they are not debarred or suspended from receiving Federal assistance. For additional information, see 44 CFR Part 17.

- Federal Debt Status. The recipient may not be delinquent in the repayment of any Federal debt. Examples of relevant debt include delinquent payroll or other taxes, audit disallowances, and benefit overpayments. (See OMB Circular A-129) (Refer to SF-424, item number 17.)

- Hotel and Motel Fire Safety Act of 1990. In accordance with section 6 of the Hotel and Motel Fire Safety Act of 1990, 15 U.S.C. §2225a, the recipient agrees to ensure that all conference, meeting, convention, or training space funded in whole or in part with Federal funds, complies with the fire prevention and control guidelines of the Federal Fire Prevention and Control Act of 1974, 15 U.S.C. §2225.

Grantees must comply with all regulations, guidelines, and standards adopted under the above statutes.

4.5 Integrating individuals with disabilities into emergency planning.
Section 504 of the Rehabilitation Act of 1973, as amended, prohibits discrimination against people with disabilities in all aspects of emergency mitigation, planning, response, and recovery by entities receiving financial funding from FEMA. In addition, Executive Order 13347, Individuals with Disabilities in Emergency Preparedness signed in July 2004, requires the Federal government to support safety and security for individuals with disabilities in situations involving disasters, including earthquakes, tornadoes, fires, floods, hurricanes, and acts of terrorism. Executive Order 13347 requires the Federal government to encourage consideration of the needs of individuals with disabilities served by State, local, and tribal governments in emergency preparedness planning.

4.6 Environmental Planning and Historic Preservation Compliance.
FEMA is required to consider the potential impacts to the human and natural environment of projects proposed for FEMA cooperative agreement funding. FEMA, through its Environmental Planning and Historic Preservation (EHP) Program, engages in a review process to ensure that FEMA-funded activities comply with various Federal laws including: National Environmental Policy Act, National Historic Preservation Act, Endangered Species Act, the Clean Water Act, and Executive Orders on Floodplains (11988), Wetlands (11990), and Environmental Justice (12898). The goal of these compliance

Appendix B: Administrative and National Policy Requirements

requirements is to protect our nation's water, air, coastal, wildlife, agricultural, historical, and cultural resources, as well as to minimize potential adverse effects to low-income and minority populations.

The grantee shall provide all relevant information to FEMA to ensure compliance with applicable Federal EHP requirements. Any project with the potential to impact natural or biological resources or historic properties cannot be initiated until FEMA has completed the required EHP review. In addition to a detailed project description that describes what is to be done with the cooperative agreement funds, how it will be done, and where it will be done, grantees shall provide detailed information about the project (where applicable), including, but not limited to, the following:

- Project location (i.e., exact street address or map coordinates)

- Total extent of ground disturbance and vegetation clearing

- Extent of modification of existing structures

- Construction equipment to be used, staging areas, etc.

- Year that any affected buildings or structures were built

- Natural, biological, and/or cultural resources present within the project area and vicinity, including wetlands, floodplains, geologic resources, threatened or endangered species, or National Register of Historic Places listed or eligible properties, etc.

- Visual documentation such as good quality, color and labeled site and facility photographs, project plans, aerial photos, maps, etc.

- Alternative ways considered to implement the project (not applicable to procurement of mobile and portable equipment)

For projects that have the potential to impact sensitive resources, FEMA must consult with other Federal, State, and tribal agencies such as the U.S. Fish and Wildlife Service, State Historic Preservation Offices, and the U.S. Army Corps of Engineers, as well as other agencies and organizations responsible for the protection and/or management of natural and cultural resources, including Federally recognized Indian tribes, Tribal Historic Preservation Offices, and the Department of the Interior, Bureau of Indian Affairs. For projects with the potential to have adverse effects on the environment and/or historic properties, FEMA's EHP review process and consultation may result in a substantive agreement between the involved parties outlining how the grantee will avoid the effects, minimize the effects, or, if necessary, compensate for the effects.

Appendix B: Administrative and National Policy Requirements

www.ingramcontent.com/pod-product-compliance
Lightning Source LLC
Chambersburg PA
CBHW080622290526

45790CB00007B/2879